WHOEVER READS THIS:

TELL ANDY KAUFMAN THAT I DON'T LIKE
THE SHOW "TAXI" AS WELL AS I USED TO SINCE
I FOUND OUT WHAT A JERK HE IS. HE MIGHT
NOT CARE WHAT I THINK OF HIM PERSONALLY,
BUT HE CAN'T BE HELPING THE SHOW'S RATINGS.

I'M IN AN ELECTRIC WHEELCHAIR AND I'D
GLADLY RUN IT OVER HIM A FEW TIMES IF IT
WOULD SHUT HIM UP, REWARD OR NO REWARD.

GOOD LUCK TO THE WOMAN--I HOPE SHE'S
AN AMAZON.

SINCERELY,
MISS LOU EVAN

Lou Evan

Selma, Indiana 47383

ANDY KAUFMAN
P.O. BOX 860
RADIO CITY STATION
NEW YORK, NEW YORK
90019

December 3, 1979

Hey! Andy Kaufman,

I got so much brains and muscle that when I finish wrestling you, you gonna look like them braided guts behind me in the picture at Acapulco's open market. I mean I'm gonna whoop your sissy-britchered, slick-haired body into a smelly pulp.

Look at my picture and tell me I can't! Why I've wrestled my six foot baby brother to the floor and tied him up with baleing cords used to tie hay with. And he begged to be let up! He was twice as big as me but that warn't make no difference to me. He needed a lesson larned.

I ain't a pretty thang to look at and I'm just as mean. When you done gone and said what you did about women, I plum got insane. You don't got no right to say us women hain't no brains to wrestle you. It don't take no brains to wrestle shit to floor! And keeping it thar ain't nothang.

Now listen hear! I'm itching to make you swallow your words live on Saturday Night'. I'm aiming for the audience and people in TV land all over America to go beserk with glee on Dec. 22 as they watch my female self conquer an IT like you. Take heed, take heed, take heed. Look at them guts in the picture again. You thank they want to be hanging thar?

I need that $1,000 to git me through some book larning at the Univ. of South Carolina. I'm working on my doctor's degree in education so you know I got a big brain. Heck, I've taught school for six years and I'm only 31 years being an old maid. Paw didn't raise no dumb childs.

Brains, muscles, I got em all. So why don't you give me a call at You oughta see me in my wrestling suit; everythang I need to whoop you is packed into that suit. Ali's Rope A Dope can't come near my wrestling technique. Mine's called, "Going down on a HALF-WIT! " That is what you is, ain't it? Scared Andy, HUH? HUH? HUH? HUH?

South Carolina 291

Dear ANDY KAUFMAN I HATE YOUR GUTS!

12-5-79   Andy
           Kaufman

Total Received   (25)

To Be Considered (2)
Rejects
                  (23)

" Rejects attached "

GE-30B(12-77)

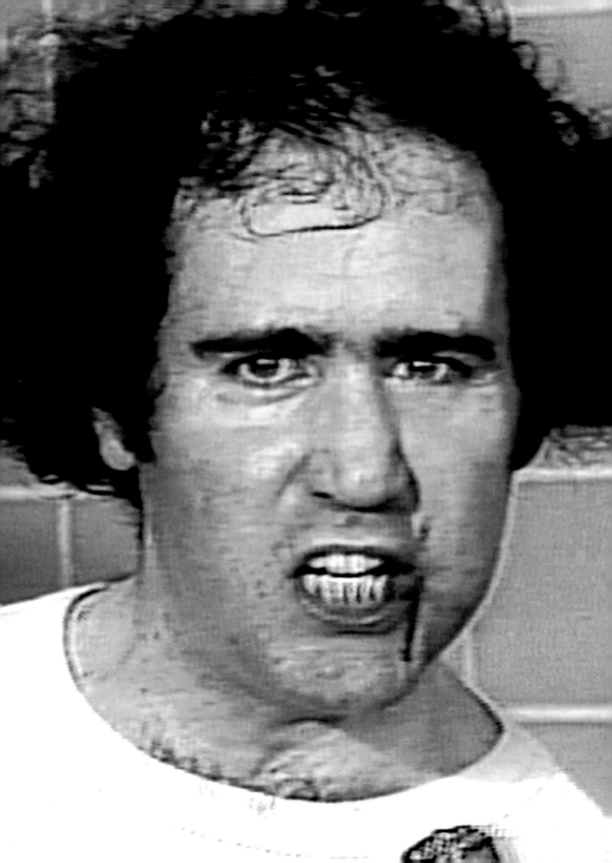

Tag Teaming with Andy Kaufman
by Bob Zmuda

I've often been asked how was it to collaborate with Andy Kaufman. What was the process like?

Well, the key was knowing his psychological imperatives. Helping to manifest those imperatives onstage was a large part of my job. Nothing illustrates this better than when Andy revealed his attraction to wrestling women.

It all started innocently enough, when I made an unannounced visit to Andy's place one afternoon. The curtains were drawn, and he took a long time to answer the door. When he finally did, I could see by the expression on his face that something was amiss. Something hidden. At first he struggled to talk about it, but then just decided to show me instead.

What he showed me was an 8mm film clip of two women wrestling in bathing suits.

A few weeks later, a few friends and I threw Andy a surprise birthday party. After Andy's arrival, I walked into his living room dressed in a referee's outfit, dragging a large wrestling mat behind me. Following me were two gorgeous girls dressed in bikinis, ready to wrestle each other for the grand prize: Andy. (Oh—and also $100, although I didn't tell the birthday boy that part.)

Two weeks later, the wrestling segment was in our road show. Three months after that, we staged it on NBC's *Saturday Night Live*. The letters started pouring in. The women hated him. Andy *loved* it.

—2009
(Bob Zmuda was Andy's writer, producer, and best friend.)

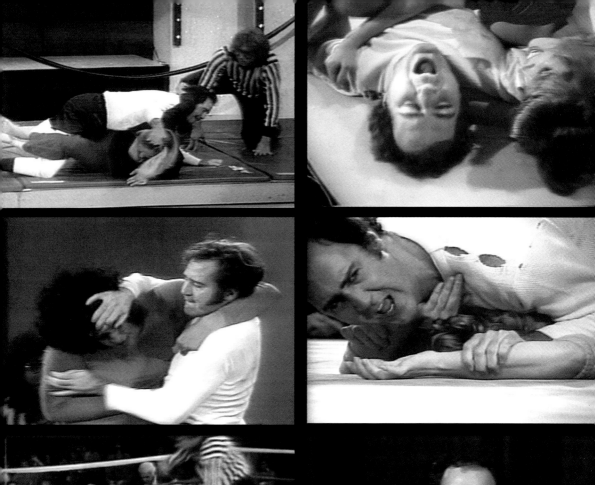

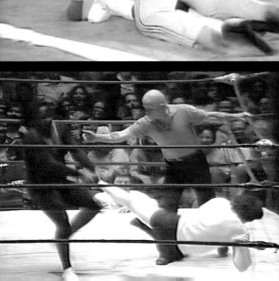

My Breakfast with Andy
by Lynne Margulies

In 1979, Andy Kaufman wrestled a woman on NBC's *Saturday Night Live* and, after disparaging the intelligence and abilities of all women, challenged women in the television audience to a similar wrestling match, offering to shave his head and pay $1,000 to the woman who could beat him. He later added that she would "get to marry him." In the following pages you'll see some of the hundreds of replies he received.

When I met Andy in 1982, he had stopped wrestling women and moved on to a larger moving target — Jerry "The King" Lawler. Andy had parlayed his intergender wrestling gimmick into a full-fledged "career" as a professional wrestler, which had been his lifelong dream. He and Lawler had already had several altercations, both verbal and physical, one of which had left Andy in a neck brace, culminating in the infamous *Late Night with David Letterman* appearance wherein Lawler gave Kaufman a tremendous slap to the floor in front of a national audience. (This is all chronicled in my documentary film, *I'm From Hollywood*.)

I came into the picture because my brother Johnny Legend had met Andy at the Olympic Auditorium in Los Angeles, where Johnny had regularly attended wrestling matches from the time he was a skinny kid — our mother would drive him there every week. Andy had come to the Olympic to meet the grand patriarch of professional wrestling, the fabulous "Classy" Freddie Blassie. Andy had idolized wrestlers since childhood; in fact, his entire act was based on the wrestler's credo of *the angrier and more rabid the audience gets, the more successful you are at your job*. Andy patterned his "bad guy" performance after 1950s East Coast wrestler "Nature Boy" Buddy Rodgers. Now that Andy lived in Los Angeles, he was out to meet his West Coast heroes. Johnny Legend and Blassie were old buddies. Freddy had recorded Johnny's songs "Pencil Neck Geek" and "Blassie, King of Men," which, it turned out, Andy had memorized, word for word.

Sometime after this meeting, Johnny and his partner, Linda Lautrec, somehow convinced Andy that it would be a great idea to do a satire on the pretentious art-house hit, *My Dinner With Andre*, calling it *My Breakfast With Blassie*. Johnny and Linda took Andy's interest at face value, put together a cut-rate crew, got a local Sambo's restaurant to agree to let them film there for free, got Fred on board and called Andy to tell him it was all set and ready to go. Amazingly, Andy showed up.

At this moment in time, I had been living in the woods in Northern California, having scorned my hometown of Los Angeles. I had no television set and hadn't stayed up to date with anything that was happening in the "outside" world, so I hadn't seen *Saturday Night Live*, *Taxi*, or any of the other shows where Andy had been famously "putting on" the entire human race. I'd never heard of the guy. But at this propitious moment, I had just decided to move back to L.A. I hadn't even unpacked my '63 Volkswagen Beetle, crammed full of my belongings, when I showed up at "the set" to see if I could be of any use.

I had long known Fred Blassie, having been raised from a pup under the auspices of Johnny Legend, who, early on, inducted me into the L.A. wrestling scene. Every week, Johnny and I watched the Olympic Auditorium matches on TV, and I was enthralled when inevitably Blassie would smash announcer Dick Lane's horn-rimmed glasses to the floor, grinding them under his heel. Johnny taught me some key wrestling moves, like the one where, with my hands planted on the floor, I kicked my legs into the air and landed my knee firmly on my opponent's throat. He took me to some of the matches at the Olympic too, so I had met Freddy when I was just a tot. But Andy Kaufman? Johnny told me (probably disgusted at my current ignorance of all things media), "Oh, he's some guy on TV."

It turned out that Sambo's had put us in their back room, and, with the place devoid of customers, Linda Lautrec, her sister Laura, Andy's friend Linda Mitchell and I were placed at a table behind Andy and Fred. We were told to "just eat and keep your voices down," so that's what we did. We forgot that they were shooting around us and just settled down to breakfast. At some point in the proceedings, Andy started talking to us with the cameras rolling, and we became active participants in the film. Somehow I ended up sitting at Andy and Fred's table for a bit and started riffing with Andy, playing off the fact that I honestly had never heard of him. We hit it off on camera, and, as it turned out, off camera as well. That was the beginning of my swift but amazing two years spent with the hurricane that was Andy Kaufman.

I quickly caught up with his career. I found his performance art amazing—right up my alley. Luckily for me, when I met him he was starting to travel regularly to Memphis to get his "revenge" on Jerry Lawler, and I went with him most of the time. Being a wrestling aficionado myself, I was having a blast. Life with Andy was crazy. We'd stay up all night going to restaurants and pinball arcades, go to bed after dawn and get up as the sun was setting. There was a period when I didn't see daylight for two weeks.

I wasn't around for Andy's intergender wrestling heyday—that happened earlier and was Bob Zmuda's territory. According to Bob, he and Andy would go through the letters he received from women challenging him to wrestle, they'd pick the cutest ones, and then Bob would book a college performance for Andy in their town.

Gee, what a coincidence! You write Andy Kaufman a letter, and soon thereafter he's performing in your town! Bob claims Andy bedded 70 percent of them. Could be true, I don't know. I do know that Andy and Bob had a blast traveling around the country together, screwing with women in both senses of the word.

So why did Andy start wrestling women in the first place? In his own words: "I'm not really a wrestler. Through the last couple of years that I've been doing it in my concerts, I've learned a lot about it by just doing it. But I wanted to recapture the old days of the carnivals...before television, you know, wrestlers used to go from town to town in carnivals and offer $500 to any man who could last in the ring with them for three minutes. So I figured if I could make it like a prize, and make it a contest, it could get very, very exciting. And it turned out to be one of the highlights, one of the most exciting parts of the concert. But I couldn't very well challenge a man in the audience, because I'd get beaten right away. I mean, most men are bigger than me, and stronger than me. So I figured if I challenged women, there are enough women who are almost as big or as big as me who would have a good chance to beat me. Whenever I play a role, whether it's good or bad, an evil person or a nice person, I believe in being a purist and going all the way with the role. If I'm going to be a villainous wrestler, I believe in going all the way with it, I believe in playing it straight to the hilt." In Bob Zmuda's words, "He wanted to get laid."

I think both are equally correct.

When Andy appeared on *Saturday Night Live*, wrestled a woman from the audience, then challenged women around the country by mocking them with, "Why don't you go back to the kitchen where you belong, wash the pots and pans, scrub the potatoes and raise the little babies," well, some women got the joke, but the majority of them hated his guts. The letters came in by the hundreds. Andy saved them all, and had them in manila folders labeled with such categories such as *Rejects* and *Possibles*. He intended to publish them in a book. Andy passed away from a rare form of cancer in 1984, and I've been lugging this box of letters around with me from home to home, storage unit to storage unit, for the past 25 years. I'm very happy to be able to finally fulfill his wish.

For more about Andy's life and art, Lynne highly recommends Bob Zmuda's book *Andy Kaufman Revealed: Best Friend Tells All*, and, of course, the aforementioned documentary, *I'm From Hollywood*, available on DVD.

Lynne Margulies is an artist and filmmaker, and was fortunate to have shared a couple of wild years with Andy Kaufman.
Very sincere thanks to Lynne's pal Dave Shulman, without whom you wouldn't be reading this.

In 1979, Andy Kaufman wrestled a woman on national television.

After verbally questioning the intelligence and abilities of ALL women, he then challenged any woman to a wrestling match, offering to shave his head and pay $1000 to the woman who could beat him.

Following are a few of the hundreds of replies he received.

Dear Andy K.,

I am the undefeated heavyweight wrestling champion of Prospect, Kentucky. The enclosed photo shows me in a recent match with the current Ohio champion (Mendel Fishberg).

As my record indicates, I am invincible. I'll pin your pig ears to the corn sty.

Love,
Cathy

The Ballad of Big D, Little E, Double B, I, E

I am woman - hear me roar
I love blood and guts and gore
Andy Kaufman is no wrestling match for me

He will see we're not all nerds
He will humbly eat his words
And he'll beg for mercy down on bended knee

When I pin him to the ground
With his cockiness unwound
We will see who scores the final victory

I am woman - hear me roar
With vigor too great to ignore
Andy Kaufman is the sure bet to concede.

December 10, 1979

To Whom It May Concern :

    I am ready to meet Mr. Kaufman's challenge. Though I have never competed in a "real" wrestling match, per se, I think you'll find me a formidable foe. I possess considerable stamina and willpower. Among my strategies is a pre-match mass consumption of garlic and the absence of bathing for two full weeks. I am hoping this will substitute any vigor I may lack.

    The $1000 winner's purse would certainly spur me on to victory since, at the present time, I am in dire straits financially. Please consider me an eager opponent and allow me to represent the women all across America who are incensed at Mr. Kaufman's arrogance. I remain,

Respectfully yours,
Debbie

Andy Kaufman
P.O. Box 860
Radio City Station
New York, NY 10019

Dear Turkey Kaufman;

I can understand why you can't find a woman who can beat you. That's because
You stick to Yankee Women. Everybody knows that all the tough broads live
down here in the deep South! There are many women here in Southern Mississippi
who could whip yo' butt, but I'm the toughest.

You might want my qualifications. I've spent the last four years of my life
building destroyers for the U. S. Navy in Pascagoula. During that time I've
been through two husbands and my electrician apprenticeship. All the guys at
the shipyard call me "Brickhouse" (or "Brick" for short). When they get fresh,
I hit them over the head with my fifty-pound tool box.

If you're serious about your offer, Cough-man, you just contact me, Sheryll
"Brick-house" Holzapfel down in the deep south!

                          Yo ASS is grass!,

                          Sheryll.

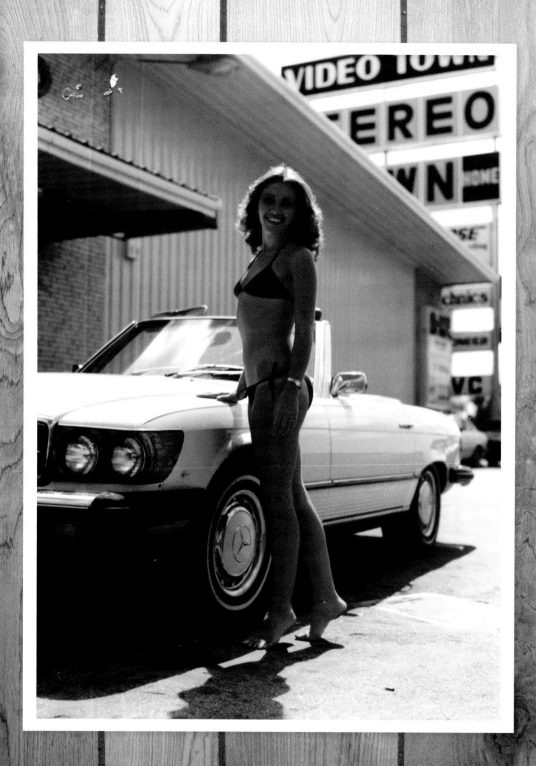

Lewisville, Texas   75056
November 26, 1979

Dear Mr. Kaufman:

On behalf of the women of America, I accept your challenge to a wrestling match. You need a lesson taught and I'm the <u>woman</u> to do it. I am a weight lifter, runner, student, mother, wife, home-maker and conqueror of male chauvinist whimps like you.

You look like a "before" picture in a Charles Atlas ad, you spineless mollusk!

I'm looking forward to December 22nd and to squashing your nose into the mat. I am prepared (above photo)! Are you?

Thank you betti much,

Debe

Debe   (Ms.)

Age: 26
Weight: 125 lbs.
Height: 5'6"
Measurements: N.O.Y.B.

November 19, 1979

Wrestle Andy Kaufman Contest

Karen R

Charlotte NC   28211

Telephone:

Statistics:
DOB: 02/04/54
HEIGHT: 5' 3½"
WEIGHT: 105 lbs.

SO Kaufman, you have called a challenge for a "match" against any
woman to take you on in wrestling. You think you are such a "macho
man" that no woman can come close to your strength. You actually
are so small minded to think that woman have no brains and are only
functional for having babies and to clean the house. Well Kaufman,
"Mr. Macho", you have met your match and I swear by the anger of
Susi Kaplow and the unshaven legs of Susan B. Anthony that I can
and will defeat you. I will prove, beyond the shadow that falls
underneath Bobby Riggs' toupee, that you are nothing more than a
spineless debased tremulous ass! I will smear your face all across
that canvas until it reflects the name of the potato dish you so
poorly portray on TV. You will eat your words Kaufman and millions
of women and men will applaud me. God, in Her grace will savor my
victory! Believe me Kaufman, when I'm through with you, you won't
be able to do your lousy imitation of Elvis because your voice will
permanently be 10 octaves higher. Yes Kaufman, you will NEVER be
able to do another gig in public again because I will totally hu-
miliate you. In essense Kaufman, you have met your match and you
are finished, i.e., el through-o!

Now, don't let my size fool you. I am one hundred and five pounds
of pure power unmatched in any form. As can be seen by the enclosed
picture I am stupendous. I am pictured here with the head of my
last opponent, Jake Jabosky. Now, Mr. Jabosky WAS a 350 pound chicken
farmer from Topeka, Kansas. He had the audacity to mock me by
wearing a chicken suit into the match to torment me. But I, the
"Unknown Wrestler" (my trademark) turned into power!!! I wrung
his neck like the chicken he really was. Needless to say I sent
his remains back to Topeka and he is now being used as feed for
pernicious hamsters. His chicken head is permanently mounted on
the front of my car as a trophy. I promise by the staples in
Larry Flint's belly button that I will do the same to you. The
"Unknown Wrestler" will be the winner. And you, will be tied by
the jock strap that is evidently to large for you and thrown out
of New York. PRAISE HER LORD! Hell, I am willing to bet that a
group of 85 year old Woman For Reagan (God knows they have to be
weak) could beat you with both hands behind their backs. You
Kaufman will be spouting the last of your malefic malediction (look
it up retard). I will destroy you.

If I'm not picked I will know that the only reason is because you
are a megalomaniaic afraid to face the truth. That's right AFRAID.
Afraid of me. Afraid to be beaten by a woman. Afraid to be seen
as a weakling before millions of Americans. You are a COWARD when
it comes to facing me and you and I both know it.

So, Kaufman Here Is YOUR CHANCE! Don't blow it. Face the"Unknown Wrestler" and learn the agony of defeat. That is if you
are man enough to take MY CHALLENGE. I will make mincemeat of
you. Your days are numbered for I and I alone will be victori-
ous!!!!!!

Signed,
The Unknown Wrestler
Karen R

To: Andy Kaufman:

I think Andy is a sissy. If
he wasn't why isn't he wrestling
men? I'm a 27 year old woman,
a mother of a three year old girl. I
know that if I can handle my daughter
he would have to be easy. If I can
pin Andy Kaufman because I am
woman enough to do the job. I
hope he has a new razor & ready to shave. I

Please man
back. That's
& just my

18

Notes from a Sensuous Woman

12/12/79

Dear Mr. Kaufman,

Enclosed please find two photo[s]
of myself taken a month ago. Yo[u]
woman can't beat you in wrestlin[g]
can and know I can. If you [want]
to try and prove your point. I [will]
definitely give you my best and [we'll]
see who comes out on top. Don't [worry]
and let the best wrestler win. I want
to prove the womans point that we are equal
[abi]lities, and I feel highly qual[ified]
[prove] this to many people.

[If you] contact me, I will be your [opponent]
and we will certainly have [a]
[real] goal time!

[If] possible, I have enclosed [a]
[my]self addred envelope to send [them]
back in. If not possible its [fine. Thank]
you for your time.

Sincerely,

Karen J.

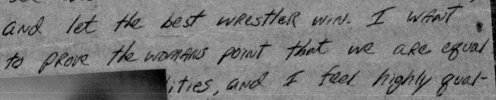

Andy,

Are you going to shave the chick's head if you beat her? That would really be something!

I've seen bald women in Porno mags and they're kind of kinky!

And then there's the slick-domed Lt. Illia in the upcoming "Star Trek" movie...

Do it! Shave her head! Shave it ALL off!!

Todd
Sylvania, Ohio

An a-Trek-tive hairdo

Former Miss India, Persis Khambatta, who won the role over nearly 100 actresses, plays Ilia, an exotic woman from another planet who joins the crew of the Starship Enterprise as a navigator in the new Paramount Pictures movie ''Star Trek: The Motion Picture.'' It will have its world premiere in Washington, D.C. on Dec. 6 and will open nationwide on Dec. 7. Playing Commander William Decker, executive officer of the Enterprise, will be Stephen Collins, who rose to screen prominence as Hugh Sloan in ''All the President's Men.'' Ms. Khambatta, a former star of Indian movies and a London fashion model, is making her Hollywood big-screen debut in this picture. She had to shave her head for her extraplanetary exploits.

Bald Women:
UNDERCOVER EROTIC FAD

88 BALD WOMEN *By T.R. Witomski.*
Nude heads may be a fad today . . . but tomorrow? Will long silky tresses go the way of mini-skirts?

LOOKS GOOD, HUH, KAUFMAN?
BE SURE TO GIVE YOUR CHALLENGER A GOOD SHAVE WHEN YOU BEAT HER! WE'RE LOOKING FORWARD TO IT — WE WANT BALD WOMEN! WE WANT BALD WOMEN!

GIVE YOU ANY IDEAS, KAUFMAN?

P.S. ASK DIANA
NIGAD TO...

Todd
Cherry Hill, N.J.

Come On, now —

Don't let me scare
you away!

here's a quarter —
: Call collect! ! !

Dear Andy Kaufman,   December 4, 1979

    As you can see by my picture I'm not
big on brains (that's why I like Saturday Night
Live) but I am big on braun. Want to
rassle a farm girl?

                        Janine

                        Bradford, N.Y. 14815

Dear Mr. Kaufman,

I heard your statement on Saturday Night Live and could not possibly believe that you think you can beat any woman in a wrestling match. You must be insane, your nothing but a scrawny little stick man. You have no meat on your body, your just flesh and bones, why I could whip you in nothing flat. So if you would like to lose your money go ahead and pick me, you male chauvenist pig you. I dare you.

Mrs. Donna (The Bruiser)

Hibbing Mn. 55746

I'd love to wrestle Andy Kaufman. It'll probably be the closest I get to a man all year.

Sincerely,
Desperate.

Desperate Doris

Marietta, Ga. 30060

TOLL FREE
(call anytime)

Season's Greetings
&
a challenge to

Stanley Kaufman, obnoxious
throwback to the Ayatollah
and Atilla the Hun.
This is Pittsburgh's answer
to the likes of you. My name
is Leyla; I am 5'10" and 150 lbs.
What you see in the picture
is the end of another friendly
housemeeting as to who gets
dish washing duty this week.
        In our cooperative the
men have evolved light years
ahead of the miscreant behavoir
you exhibit. Evolution is
on my side, you creep.
                See ya'
                        Leyla

Pgh. PA. 15206

KOFMANN—

LOWED
S OF
TS, BE
ALING
I'M
NDERS
N THE
E STAGE
2EY.
YOU
TNG
E
S T

the dog.

Please find inclosed a photograph taken after your inane proposal. RSVP

att...
...
mo...

a m...
bit...
kee...
tou...
in S...

four
Durin
ship
).

t co...

OL... ART
A ...SER
IR...
IE...
U...
CO...
TH...
PREY.

UK
TT...
ANC...
UN...

iou...
a...
ity...

I challenge you to

let it scare

lucky if you can even pick yourself

PERSONAL MANAGEMENT
PAUL CANTOR ENT. LTD
174 S. BEVERLY DRIVE
BEVERLY HILLS, CA. 9

BOBBIE

Nov. 19

Dear Andy Kaufman,

The show I am with can't get work — so now I'm in L.A. Considering the straight life. It stinks.

I work from 6 a.m. to 10 a.m. in a donut shop. From 11 a.m. to 5 p.m. in a department store selling books. I work from 7 a.m to 6 p.m. on Saturdays and Sundays in a dog kennel shoveling ka-ka. — The whole enchilada at 3 bucks an hour. After taxes that comes to about 9.ºº a week.

Who am I kidding?

I'd wrestle the Loch Ness monster for a chance to get outta this.

Besides, my parents live in New Jersey and it would be a chance to be home for the first time in over a year. Christmas away is soul-shattering

Dear Mr. Koffman,

I watch Taxi every night on Tuesday. And I was watching Saturday Night Live, and I heard your remark about Ladies

being stupid and couldn't fight, well I might be 11 years old but I chalenge you and me in a fighting ring together and I whip you so bad I'll teach you ≡ to keep your smart ≡ mouth shut about wemon. But I heard you say the first ladie to beat ~~you~~ fighting you will get $1000 and if

I beat you fighting
all but that money
in my school ed.
Here is a picture of
me, just like you ordered

Sincerely,
Rita Sherman

Kaufman you miserable wimp,

　　Despite your obviously degenerate genetic characteristics
the obscenely flabby state of your physical body, you talk a v
brave fight out there before the TV cameras, protected as you
by the studio security personnel that guard you from the right
　　　　　　　　　　　　　　Some of us know the truth, thou
　　　　　　　　　　　　　　rooftops, to denounce you

I WON!!!
(12-22-79)

... ⊙#!¢, She
MADE MY head
Split into two AND
NOW I Look LiKe
that guy FROM TAXi...
... OWie... OH, HERE
COME the CLiPPERS...
I quit show business
... WhO AM I ¢ where
am I, OWie

To Andy - You Pig

I am woman -
you're a bore
and I'll pin you t
and I'm so rough
you once again.
'Cause I heard you
and I don't wanna
to your woman s
gonna put an end

Dear Andy,

　　WRESTLiNg You wiLL be
LiKe counTing Sheep. If
I can beat "Gumby" I can
beat You!!!!!!!!!!!!!!!!!!
Your FRiend!!!!!!

34

yah! Andy ↓ P.S. I was even a mean baby.

My name is Lady Pepper

My address is Wichita, Kansas 67214

Andy is a ...

" AS MY INSTR

C'MON ANDY I Dare Ya.

Kaufman -
I must say that, after seeing your announcement, via sattelite, I would enjoy nothing more in this entire galaxy than to come to the defense of all female species by pulverizing you on nationwide T.V.

I will be residing at the above address with some dear Earth friends by the time this arrives to you, but give me just one phone call, you creep, and I will be on the next flying apparatus to New York. I am:

.21000 ions (23 earth years of age)
108 belzoons (5 foot 5 inches in height)
27¾ shmaltzlas (118 pounds)

my record:
· undefeated at Remulac High
· undefeated in Remulac Junior College
· undefeated so far this year (Powder-Puff Wrestling Team)

Hope you have the guts to take me on -
Laurie

Hey! Kaufman!

I know I can pin you! Why? Because I don't think you have the brains to pin me!

At your recent Seattle concert, I went up on stage hoping to be chosen to pin you (notice the positive attitude), but I was not picked. That's okay It wasn't in the stars.

So when you came on "Saturday Night Live" with invitation to females, it opened up another opportunity to whip yo' ass.

November 21, 1979

Saturday Night Live
c/o Andy Kaufman --Wrestling
P.O. Box 860
Radio City Station
New York, New York   10019

Dear Mr. Kaufman,

Nothing could be more tasteless _____ on the
Dinah Shore Show, so your wrestling women does not surprise
me as being tasteless. I think your best opponent would be
Dinah Shore as she would probably love to pound a few lumps
in your head. Alas, I know that that is not possible as she
is too old and you're not as good looking as Burt Reynolds.

Therefore, I know that I AM THE opponent to fight you. I
will represent her in behalf of the abused middle aged women
in this country. I am 28 years old, but I really "feel" for
women over 40 because women are considered over the hill once
they reach 40 in our society. Personally, I think you're a
woman hater and a chauvinist pig.

I will wrestle you ANYWHERE -- ANYTIME. I will challenge you
in a kitchen. I will put your head in a meat grinder or else
in a microwave oven so your brain will explode inside out.
Maybe we could knead some bread or roll out pie dough as to
see who is the strongest physically. It takes a lot of
strength and stamina to do this. No, I am not a sicky. I
am a respected dental assistant. You are cute by the way,
even if you are a sadistic moron.

If this is a real honest to goodness wrestling match, please
feel free to contact me --

                    Ann   Phone #:

              Worth, Illinois 60482   (suburb of Chicago)

Please keep my name confidential, I'd rather be known as
Tootsie Larooski. I'm very proud of my Polish heritage.

Regards,

Tootsie

Enc.

Mr. Andy Kaufman,
 i accept your wrestling
challenge. Of course, i
can cook up a 10-course
meal with my left hand,
while i dust off the frame
of my P.h.d. with my right
hand and scrub the kitchen

floor with my feet. But
i can wrestle! Woman
are naturally better
at wrestling than men,
and i am the meanest,
brainiest woman to
ever wield a pan. Even
panless, i'll take you
down in a matter of
seconds. Now that i've
accepted your challenge,
can you accept mine?

Sheila

ALTHOUGH I'M ONLY 5'7",
115 lbs. AND CUTE AS A BUTTON,
I CAN BEAT HIM BECAUSE I HAVE
STOMACH HAIR! THESE ARE NOT
YOUR EVERYDAY STRANDS, BUT
WILD AND KRAZY HAIRS. I CAN
KEEP THAT NURD-FACE OFF THE
VIDEO-WAVES FOR GOOD, NO SWEAT.

SHERRY

SAN JOSE, CA. 95129

st for a female wrestlin
ndously insulting commen
avior I could not turn
a lesson.

to wrestle me, Sarah Bea
22, 1979. Have a razor
d and

Dear
Black
Wrest
Studer
Said

December 10, 1979

Mr. Andy Kaufman
P.O. Box 860
Radio City Music Hall
New York, New York 100

Dear Mr. Kaufman:

Yes. I am one of those women who lifts weights---one
of those women who also has an adverse reaction to men
who tend to be what one might call "terribly male-defined".
I can relate to that, though, as I define myself along
those same lines. But it's okay for a woman, you see.

I have a sense of humor, unlike most "radical feminists".
I am also very attractive.

So, Andy, if you want to fight, I could hold you down---
you know, get out a bit of my stored-up anger. I could
also get a few laughs (at your expense, of course).

In any case, I've had experience playing before crowds.
Take that any way you like. I love attention, applause,
and wrestling (the latter, with women).

I'll take you, Kaufman. Anything's worth a shot. Hey,
I live right down the street ...

COLLEGE OF OSTEOPATHIC
MEDICINE AND SURGERY
DES MOINES IOWA

Dear Andy Kaufman —
You were cute as a
Robut Butler, funny as a
Check Taxi Driver, But now
you are outright profound as the
"Male Whiplash." You may simply be
doing your stchick but I find the
message long overdue.

Todays Man's problem with womens
Lib is simply, As men we've been
Liberalized into being Pusswads.

What Todays Man fails to
realize is that the Traditional
male/female roles were not developed
by shear Accident or out of evil
plot to subordinate women. Rather
This is the result of several
million years of Natural selection.
As useual Modern Man is learning
(just As her has with pollution) what
folly it is to fuck with Mother
Nature.

Medical Science has long known That
There are definate physiological differences
between The male/female Brains.

Any student of human behavior will
readily Admit That There Are striking
variances in male/female behavior —
it simply Ain't all Socialized.

Modern man hAS TAkinG quite
an unfair beating at The hands
of feminists. I am glad That you
have demonstrated The guts To voice
your somewhat True but whimisical
statement of Todays woman.

In short — Thank you for
stepping foward — And beAT The
hell out of That girl for
MANkinds Sake.

Sincerely,
Ron

broad
POWER

If I'm chosen, I'll do
my very best.
            Sincerly,
            Vicki

Vicki

Baltimore, Maryland
                212.05
5'11" 135 lbs   21 yrs. old

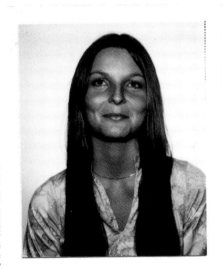

"Dear Andy,
        you haven't wrestled
till you wrestle the "cleveland
cruncher" Esther Shuster.

                    Good luck!

        K.
UNIVERSITY HTS., OH 44118

ANDY KAU
BE

I ACCEPT
YOUR
CHALLENGE!

MAN
WARE

CLEVELAND

OU'VE GOT TO BE TOUGH!

BE WATCHING.

VITA

Esther Schuster

Cleveland, Ohio 44118

SIGN   Scorpion   **AURA**   Very Pretty

BIRTH   Born to poor unspecting immigrant parents in the small town of Buffalo N.Y., 1951

HEIGHT   From 21 inches to 66½ inches

WEIGHT   7 lbs. 2 oz to 140 lbs.

EYE COLOR   Hazel

OCCUPATION   Psychiatric Social Worker

December 15, 1979

Mr. Andy Kaufman
Radio City Station
Box 860
New York, New York
10019

Dear Mr. Kaufman:

Esther Schuster, (Cleveland so-
cial-worker), would like to meet
your wrestling challenge. She
has two towel boys and sponsors.

Cleveland needs a boost and this
is just what we need.

Please consider Esther Schuster.

Thank you.

Jacqueline

Jacqueline

A DAY IN THE LIFE

OF
ESTHER SCHUSTER

Sensitive, thoughtful, at peace with the world........ spaced out !

Bright, young intellectual... studying
mind control and the supernatural

.... On her way to the gym

Andy Kaufman,

I challenge

YOU

I am 5'4" and ___
(and 27 years old)
I believe I could successfully
defeat Mr. Kaufman. For the past
three years I have been a nurse
on the orthopedics ward of a hospital,
really building up my muscles slinging
those casts, wheelchairs, and patients
around. I have also had to restrain
psychiatric patients which would be
very helpful in Mr. Kaufman's case.
Also, if I should lose, I already
know how to use crutches.
                    I'm enclosing a

Mr Kaufman,   19 Nov 79
    My Name is Dianna   - Oklahoma City
And The Other Pictured in Black, pink+
Green is Sonja   of Arkansas.
    Were   Soilders in the U.S. Army.
W Charlies → Truck Drivers. Stationed
At   Fort Lewis, WA. 9th S+T Bravo. Co.
What I'm Trying to Say is,
Not only Can I cook, Sew,
Have Babies And Make love.
    I Can Shoot My M46 Day
or Night And Not miss my target!
Also I Can woop Ass on
you on any of my Bad Days!
And I don't ever have A good one!
Think About it FATTY!

                                                  57
```
```
         IS I CAN'T

Nov. 18, 1979

Dear Andy

I want to know ~~if~~ if
11 eleven year old kids can
wrestle you. Because this
chance may never come back
so don't go back in your
den come back out and
fight a 11 year old ~~big~~ boy
if you have the guts.

From the: hills

Nov. 22/79

To: Andy Kaufman,
    your an old fashioned
fogey. Give me a chance
and I could wrestle you
and win, until you cry and
plead with me for mercy.
    I am a punk woman,
and I intend to over take you.

        Diane "Teazer"

        Unionville, Ontario,
        Canada, L3R-1A6

(Toronto)

NAme: SHAWNA
ADDRESS:
                Youngstown, Ohio
Occupation: VOCALIST & Designing FASHion
Height: 6'
Weight: 146

19 November, 1979

Dear Mr. A. Kaufman,

    I know you only asked for women to write in but you are only showing that you're just a "Fag." Men already know that they are smarter than women. Aren't you man enough to challenge another man, or maybe you were a woman at birth and had a sex transplant?

    I challenge you to a wrestling match. Are you one of those guys who think they are macho but are just a "Big Pussy" in realty. I would like to know how you can call yourself a "Man?" (Answer my questions on the next show if you're man enough to "FAG BAIT?") Why don't you and your friends (Fags) go back into hiding? If, you're man enough, you will accept my challenge, and if you do not

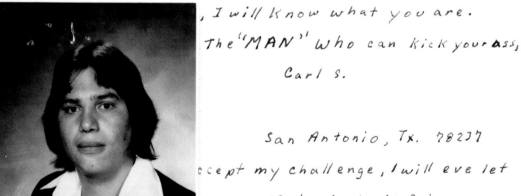

, I will know what you are.
    The "MAN" who can kick your ass,
    Carl S.

    San Antonio, Tx. 78237
ccept my challenge, I will eve let
our purse to make it fair.
   , HA, HA, HA.

Andy Kaufman
P.O. Box 860
Radio City Station
New York, N.Y.
10019

Dear Mr. Kaufman,

With no formal training in physical culture, but with brains to spare, I know I can beat you wrestling.

I am a high school English teacher, feminist, union activist, Bob Dylan fan, entrepreneur in the combat zone.

I stand five feet tall, weigh about 100 pounds. 'lbs all strength. You can see from recent photos that I can look like a pussycat — or — the real me.

Saturday nite Live would have to pay all my expenses but I'm willing to forfeit the $1000.00

victory money just for the glory of
defeating you.

I am married, have no children
(none planned or on the way), am thirty-seven
but look younger. I'm a natural blond
with blue eyes. My measurements have
been the same for years: 32-24-34.
I'm in good health, excellent fighting
condition.

Because I also have stage
presence and a good sense of
humor, I could smooth over your
disgruntlement at losing, with
some clever, yet soothing remarks.

Even though you will lose, I'll
still be your fan, as I have been
since first I saw you.

I'm the one !!!!

Kristy J

home:
work:

DEC 4, 1979

I Think i can WRESTLE ANDY
KAUFMAN. Cause i can BEAT &
Rip up any old guy. No maTTER
who. I will geT him & Rip him up
So good. THAT HE can'T EAT, SLEEP,
TalK OR WalK AnyMORE. So IF I
am THE ONE who will BE on
SATURDAY night LIVE REMEMBER
KAUFman i will CREam you good.
give me any body i will seT
Them good i am a REAL good FighTER

s
g/b
ose
cl

a
s
nd
r

ld
t
en
nn
re

rs
s
an
re
un
e
her

Vens
not
got

Good Humor Corporation

800 SYLVAN AVENUE • ENGLEWOOD CLIFFS, NEW JERSEY 07632 • TEL. 567-8000

Linda

Northridge CA 91325

Andy Kaufman
PO Box 860
Radio City Station
New York, New York 10019

Dear Andy:

Using a utilitarian philosophy, your choice on who to fight ought
to result in producing the greatest good for the greatest number of
people. Thus, you should fight me. You see, people have been trying
to beat me up, or generally do away with me for 19 years. You would
promote utility by bringing happiness to all these people. Since I'm
only 5'4" and a scarce 92 pounds, one quick punch could do it.

It is hard to say how many people you would bring pleasure to by
fighting me. They range from several schoolyard bullies, to nurses
who would purposefully break needles in me, to firemen who rescued my
cat but left me in the tree. And those are just the ones I know of;
there are countless others I have never discovered.

Even my parents consistently tried to get rid of me. As the
articles I've inclosed show, my family seemed to misplace me as often
as possible.

I've been fighting back all this time, which has begun to weigh
heavily on my conscience. I offer you a chance to bring happiness to
many, and help me to be at peace with my philosophy.

Sincerely,

Linda

Linda

Los Angeles—An infant girl
crawled safely to her hom
yesterday after being mis
ing for four months. Lit
Linda   was reporte
missing last July 12th, f
the home of Mr. and Mrs.
Ralph Lenhoff in metropoli
Los Angeles. According to
the child's mother, Tessie
the infant was last seen
securely seated in a play-
pen in the   's back
yard. "Then I turned aroun
and noticed that the gate
was unlatched and the dog
was gone." Police contend
that either Linda followed
the dog out, or that she
was dragged out by the har-
ness leash she sometimes
shares with the dog.

Doctors report that
Linda survived on berries,
earthworms, and "other thing
she picked up in the gutter."
Also found stuck to the
baby's clothes were several
small steak bon

An atypic
g incider
ay, when
rned to
opping i
Wednesda
by a mar
onsequer
ughter,
ays told
purse
," said
ed my p
a went
im."
n, art:
er four
d chec
a smal
little
bin, s
e was u
ad bee
Later
o sai
skinny
block

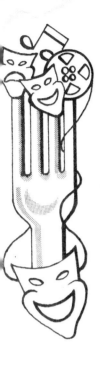

⦿⦿⦿⦿⦿⦿"Fork"⦿⦿⦿⦿⦿⦿

West Seneca, New York 14224
November 23, 1979

Andy Kaufman
P.O. Box 860
Radio City Station

Andy,

I won't dignify you by a salutation with a 'dear' in it! I
want to wrestle you on television. I was born and reared on
farms all of my life. I have been dealing with 'animals' all
of my life. I have slopped and wrestled with pigs on many
occasions. It would be nothing new to wrestle one more "pig"
on television...I would even give you the advantage of greasing
your body, although you appear to be greasy enough as it is!
By the way, I don't have three-heads, it's just a picture!

In training to whip your _____,

Shawne M

Shawne M.

— I **know** that _I_ can beat _YOU_, Andy Kaufman, at wrestling **because** _I am_ much, _MUCH_, _MUCH_, smarter than _YOU_ !!!!oooo _I_ am going to a _UNIVERSITY_ to become an _ANIMAL BEHAVIORIST_ — NOT a _COMEDIAN_ (cheap, boo-hiss's), therefore _I KNOW_ I can & WILL beat _YOU_ !!!!!!oooooo I am, also, **better** than you! What do you say to that oo! Women are NOT, I repeat NOT, made for the kitchen, housework, etc!oo Women are EQUAL, if not BETTER, than MEN — especially MALE CHAUVINIST PIGS like yourself oo! So - just challenge me — I DARE YOU, because I AM NOT AFRAID, ARE YOU ????—

Love & happiness,
Carolyn R.

Age 16

Houston, Texas
77035

P.S. I am & going to be BETTER than you ARE, HAVE BEEN, OR EVER

I hope you hAVE Alot of money BecAuse I'm shore there's Alot of women ot there who CAn Kick your Butt.

and Address

You Stink Andy

325 lbs. Can't stand superior thinking, male chauvenist pig types.

Hey Jerk!
ALL men stink - especially you! I don't think you can beat me because I would pin you in the first round. I don't need to Lift weights because the only thing I need to Lift is your hair in a bag and $1000. You better send me that plane ticket real soon. You think you're real tough but you won't be so tough when I finish with you. So you ...ket fast

Nov. 18th

Dear Mr. Kaufman,

I could beat you in Any
wrestling match, once on week
days and twice on Sunday. The
REASon I'd like to wRestle you is
so I can prove to you that
women have more brains than
men do! I'm 18 years old, 5'ft
6"in. tall And weigh 210 lb

I work out daily with
bells And you said you wo
even take on the ones th
did that, too. Hope to hear
you soon!
                    Sincerly,
                         Becky

Andy Kaufman,
    I agree that men can take most woman,
but I'm tired of hearing you shoot of
your mouth and I think it's time
some one shut you up. Your a nice
person, but you have one hell of a mouth.
I challange you to a wrestling match.
Little ole me against you.

                         Sincerly

11-17-79

79

12-4-79

Dear Andy;

I can beat you because of an infamous
wrestling hold I use. The Tickler.

And I would love to see a man "Kauf" -
up $1,000, and get the shaving of his
life.

You'll need an ambulance to taxi you
off the stage when the match is over.

Have a good day.

Sincerely,

Rita

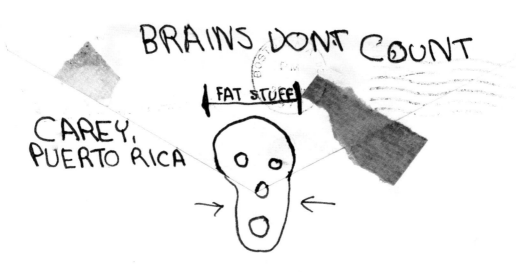

BRAINS DONT COUNT

← FAT STUFF →

CAREY,
PUERTO RICA

FORGET THE RITHER

I kin WHOP th'
livin' **** outta
you but you're too
Cute to die.

P.S. Tell Gilder ta
Give ya what ya
deserve

W.L.

Becky

HOW SWEET iT iS To HAVE a FRIEND LiKE YOU...

11/18/79

DEAR MR. KAUFMAN,
    YOU ARE AN
INANE DRONE..
BEING A RATHER ATTRACTIVE YOUNG
lAdy of twenty, I hAVE, of
necessity, become an expert
WRESTLER. Therefore, I hereby
ACCEPT YOUR CHALLENGE, And
MORE OVER, will pin YOU in
SIXTY SECONDS.

                    SINCERELY,
            Rebecca A.

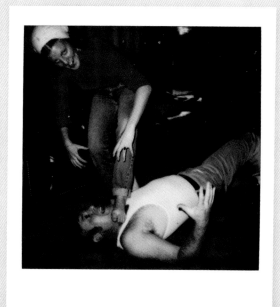

Katherine

Dear Andy,
I'm beautiful, smart, & kind.
The best you're gonna find.
If it's your mind you're gonna use,
it's your behind you're going to lose!

Statistics
Age: 30   Weight: 110 lbs
Height: 5 ft. 4 in.   Married: 2 children
Measurements: 37-25-36

Dear Mr. Kauffman,
I can beat you
in wrestling! My qualifications
are being a housewife and
a mother of three boys
that I wrestle from dawn
to dusk. And believe me
I don't have ordinary
boys. My oldest has to
grow just a foot a three
inches And he'll be as
tall as me, And hes just
six yrs. old! I'll wrestle
you! I'm 25 yrs. 5'3½",
blonde, brown eyes, weigh
118 lbs. come on
you're on!

P.S. Besides I can
use the vacation!

Gigi

I DARE YOU!!

I am Chai Voris, Terre Haute, Ohio's (Pop. 20)
most experienced Wrestler. I think I have wrestled
just about every man in Terre Haute and I have "Beat
the Pants Off" every one of them. Does Mr. Andy Kaufman
think he is any different than any other Man?

I say HA!

                    And HA HA HA!

                              (And since it's close to
                                Christmas) HO HO HO!!!

I know by day I may look like a meek and mild
Secretary, but by night...

                    Look out Men! Here I Come!

I dare Andy Kaufman to wrestle me, or is he afraid
of becoming one of my statistics (and another run in my
Panti-hose.)

                         Signed,
                         The Chai-d Lady
                         The Chai-d Lady

Dear Mr. Kaufman,
   I am challenging you to a
wrestling match Because I _know_
that I am _mentally_ _much more_
superior to you, even though you
are probably _double_ my weight and
triple my age. I weigh 98 pounds
and am 14 years old. I _like doing_
easy things.

                    Your Challenger,

                    Leslie

November 17, 1979

Dear Mr. Kaufman,   11/18/79

I'm writing to you in response to the wrestling
challenge you made on Saturday Night Live
November 17, 1979. I am 6'0" and weigh 180 lbs.
and was a competitive swimmer for thirteen years.
I take great pride in my size and strength and like
to show it off whenever I get the chance. The
only problem is that the chance doesn't come up very
often since most people don't get into wrestling unless
its a local, district, state, national or international
championship match. People would rather drink, eat
and socialize at parties than wrestle. I'm a very
competitive woman and enjoy proving to the opposite
sex that I am just as good and 9 times out of 10
much better than they are in anything they want to
challenge me with. And now, getting back to your
wrestling challenge. I know I can whip you Mr.
Kaufman, and besides, I think you and I would put
on a great show.

                              Sincerely,
                              Barbara Diane
                              New York, New York 10036
                              Tel:

I want to wrestle Andy Kaufman
because I look like a Woman,
act like a Lady, think like a man,
and could beat that sucker.

Cindy,
are you serious? My grandmother could do
it! Besides, anyone who looks like   waxxa wrestle
...tn (son of sam), has got   augh is enough
you to   xg to face
know I'll win   e humiliation?
    x an aver ripe
    . Do you
    ut don't! Sometimes
    want

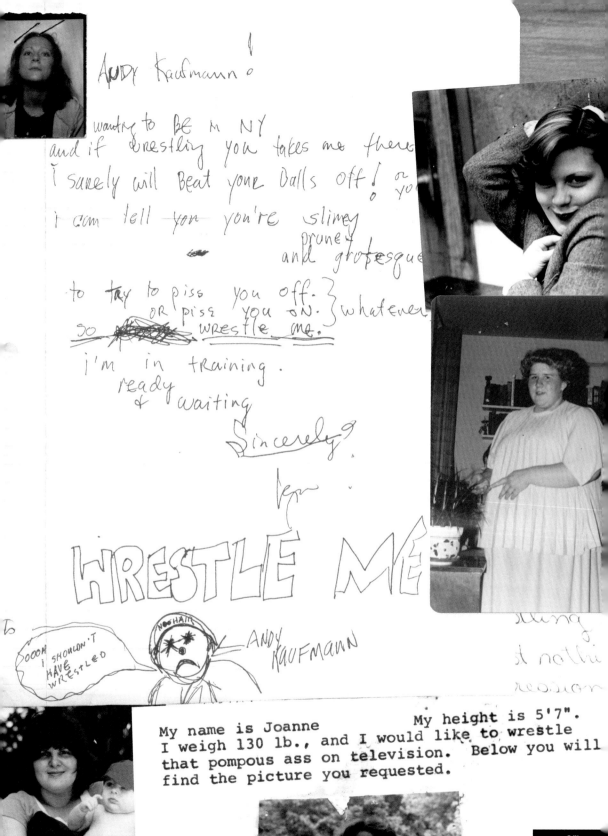

ANDY Kaufmann!

wanting to BE in NY
and if wrestling you takes me there
I surely will Beat your Balls off! or you.
i can tell you you're slimey
                    pruney
                and grotesque
to try to piss you off.} whatever
       or piss you on. } whatever
so ~~xxxxx~~ WRESTLE me.

i'm in training.
  ready
    & waiting
        Sincerely,

          ~~kim~~

WRESTLE ME

OOOH i SHOULDN'T HAVE WRESTLED   NO HAIR   ANDY KAUFMANN

My name is Joanne   My height is 5'7".
I weigh 130 lb., and I would like to wrestle
that pompous ass on television. Below you will
find the picture you requested.

Dear Mr. Kaufman

I would like the money that I am going to win, to take care of my family. I have been russle for 6 years with my Brothers, So I can Beat you easily. your chances of winning are Very Very slim So if i get to russle you i will Beat the hall out of you. and if you don't pick me i will sick my ~~heavy wait~~ cousin p.g. after you.

Sincerly yours

Nancy Woodside

me !

P.S. I am only ten.

11/17/79

Andy Kaufman
P.O. Box 860
Radio City Station
NYC, NY 10019

Dear Andy,
     You ask why I think I can beat you in a wrestling match? The answer is simple . . .

I AM WOMAN

Linda

November 19, 1929

DEAR ANDY:

You sexist jerk! I'm going to rip your lungs out! I'll give you a traechotomy with my BARE HANDS! I'm going to RE-Arrange your face so badly that when you feel the urge to pick your nose you'll scratch your ear lobes! I'll see you in N.Y. on Dec. 22. P.S. my vital stats are 5'2" & 110 pounds of Shit kicking fury, sucker.

SUE

WEST LINN Oregon
97068

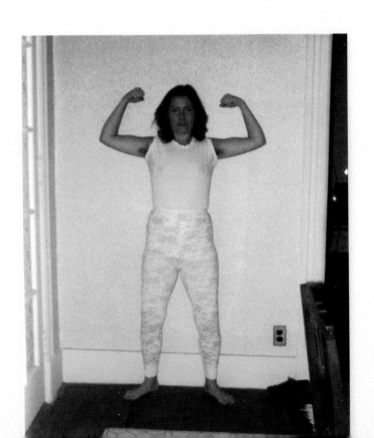

Dear Mr. Kaufman,

with one hand tied behind
my back. I, myself, coming
from an Orthodox Jewish home,
will personally sit shiva for
you when I'm through! I
look forward to pinning your
ass on the Christmas show,
If you're man enough to
challenge me personally.

Sincerely,

Matt

Colo. Spgs. Color

In this corner is Millie "the Mauler"
...ever standing 5'2" a...
As a teen I spe...
...my brother...

playp...

...3/3/79

...p like you. I'll give
...have my head if you
...that frail body of
...ore, you are a no-tal
...de it out of luck.
...rring in "Taxi"-why
...one? someone with
...ld fit in perfectly

...ent of T...
...aufman
...club

Andy Kaufman

: Because this will prove I will put yo...
your place, the gutter! This will pro...
made man first than made woman,
learned from his mistakes! This will pr...
that any woman can keep any man in h...
place, This will prove that you are b...
Also I'll give you a run for your money

mypis...

ndy

...andle this ...
...man call:

Susanne
25yrs old   5'5"   125lbs
professional model / singer / actress.

I have just recently arrived here from England
and I found this persons comments rather
offensive. If it is at all possible I would be
most willing to sort him out by means of a
wrestling bout.

Thank you,

Susanne

Woodside
Queens.

Inside Kung Fu Magazine   13 December 1979

Hollywood, Ca. 90028

GRACIELA
(personality profile)

age: 23   Height: 5'4   Weight: 120

Andy Kaufman Challenge
    Last July, on Friday the 13th, a former beauty queen defeated
the reigning champ to become the Womens' Bantamweight Boxing Champ-
ion of the World. Graciela Casillas, once the city of Oxnard Miss
Latin America, has a professional ring record of 14-1-0 with 12 KO's.
Her world title is recognized by the World Womens Boxing Association
(WWBA).
    Miss Casillas is also a perfessional Karate Champion. Within
the next few months, she will fight for the Women's Bantamweight
Karate Championship of the World, sanctioned by the World Karate
Association (WKA). At this time, Miss Casillas is expected to become not only the first woman, but the first American to win two
pugilistic World Championships. WKA title bouts, such as hers, are
frequently covered by NBC-TV. Miss Casillas has already appeared on
NBC's Real People.
    Besides the contrast between her feminine grace and her athletic
career, what makes Graciela Casillas an enigma is her highly cultur-
ed background. Miss Casillas is a Masters' candidate in Educational
Psychology at California State University at Northridge.
    Speaking as the editor of the second largest Martial Arts Maga-
zine, I can personally atest that Graciela Casillas is the genuine
article...a World-Class Champion. Enclosed are some photos of Miss
Casillas as well as feature articles from Boxing and Martial Arts
publications. She may be reached at   Mountain
View, Ca. 94042——or by leaving a message with me,
between 9:00-11:00 a.m. (EST), or   between 11:00-8:00
p.m. (EST).

                                        Sincerely,

                                        Paul

                                        Paul
                                        Editor
                                        Inside Kung Fu Magazine

Nov. 27 1979

DEAR ANDY,

I SAW "SAt. Night LivE" ON NOV. 17 IN WHICH YOU CHALLANGED ANYONE to BEAT YOU IN A WRESTLING MATCH.

IF I HAD tHE CHANCE I KNOW tHAt YOU WOULD BE NO MAtCH FOR MY STRENGtH, BOtH INtELLECtUALLY AND PHYSICALLY.

I WATCHED YOO OFTEN ON tHE DICK VAN DYKE SHOW AND BELIEVE YOO to BE A POOR EXAMPLE OF tHE MALE RACE. I tHINK YOUR STATEMENT IN WHICH YOU SAID YOU COULD BEAT ANY WOMAN IN A MATCH IS VERY IDEALISTIC.

I CAN'N'T BELIEVE YOU, ANDY, HAVE THE GALL TO PROFESS YOUR SUPERIORITY TO WOMEN ON NATIONAL T.V.

I lOVE WRESTLING. THE BEST BOUT I HAVE EVER SEEN WAS IN THE 1972 Olympics IN WHICH ALEKSADR MEDVED OF THE U.S.S.R. WON THE SUPER HEAVY WEIGHT title IN WRESTLING.

I'm 27 YEARS OlD AND THE MOTHER OF ONE CHILD. I'm 5'3", 318 POUNDS, AND MY Stats ARE 56-70-78½. I BELIEVE IF GIVEN THE CHANCE I WOULD POUNCE YOU to A PUlp. I CHALLENGE YOU to PROVE YOUR MASCULINITY.

SINCERELY,
Joanne.

Detroit, MI
48230

Peggy

L.A. Calif 90027
home phone:

Age: 30   36-26-36
                measurements
Height: 5' 7"
Weight: 130 lbs

Dear Andy Kaufman:

I accept your challenge to wrestle you on "Sat. Night Live". I had never wrestled before, but when I heard you say that you thought a woman could not beat you because of intelligence, I had to respond. I am not trained in any martial arts or physical combat of any kind. I am a mother of an eight year old boy.

But my intelligence is not limited in the way you expressed. I know I am smart enough to pin you down. I will win, not because I am big or strong, but because I am smarter than you. I can anticipate your moves, and move faster than you. I, in turn, challenge you. Do you accept? Or are you looking for someone you can more easily over come? I am the one who can beat you, Andy Kaufman. Do you dare? Sincerely - Peggy

L.A. Calif 90027

TAMMIE TEMPTATION   "MISS NEROTICA"

Brooklyn, New York, 1201
December 12, 1979

Dear Andy Kaufman —

I would personally like to accept your challenge to women for a fair fight on television. I'm ready to prove my sex is superior to yours.

Don't be fooled by my size. I have the strength of ten men. Number eleven I tell to get lost. You won't be the first man I've laid out flat. I've had bigger and stronger men than yourself on their knees before me begging for mercy.

I can take men three at a time and leave them gasping and writhing on the floor, so I don't think little old you will be any problem for me.

I hope you will accept my challenge to meet on the mat.

Yours truly,
Tammie Temptation

November 21, 1979

Mr. Andy Kaufman
P.O. Box 860
Radio City Station
New York, NY 10019

Dear Mr. Kaufman:

This letter is in answer to your challenge on the November 17th episode of Saturday Night Live. Enclosed are several photographs of myself. One would not tell the story. They are numbered for your convenience.

Number 1. I'll be honest with you from the start because I'm sure you can tell from the photo that I'm a late bloomer. This was taken at age 21 when I became a brownie scout.

Number 2. This one was taken at age 40 just after returning from an expedition to Central Africa in search of a youth serum said to be used by a twenty-thousand year old tribe of marmoset pigmies. We found the serum and barely escaped with our lives.

Number 3. This was, believe it or not, taken two weeks ago at age 88. As you can see, the serum side effects wore off and it really did work. Believe me, to be able to look like I do now, at 88 years old; it was worth every minute of the 22 years I spent working as a marmoset at the Miami Zoo.

Well, if you think you can really handle a wrestling match with someone with a background like mine, just let me know. I should be up your way in the next few weeks. I have an aunt that I owe a visit. She's working her way through Columbia as a pidgeon in Central Park.

See you soon.

Linda

P.S. Actual birthdate=
     March 27, 1953

Durham, NC 27712

Andy,
   I want to wrestle you be- cause you a <u>fat</u> M.C.P. and a C.B. (CRASHING BORE) besides. Women are good for <u>a lot</u> of things besides washing ing th I kno cret, obv takes strength wouldn't

self an inteligent woman a battle of witts with 'ike fighting an unarmed being a male chauvini good for is taking out th the dishes and walking

'osed a pho   n 30¢
          roposal.

TAKE IT
OUT HARD

s hole th
nly to
our fat
and yo
wrestl
T.V.!

Duh... I chalenge youse to a wrestle. Awm numma one, so done forget it buddy. Wildcat woman is out for blood. Lemme tangle wid ya.

Mr Kaufman
I'd like to take a couple of punches at ya turkey. (or is it chicken or little ol

DEAR ~~ASSHOLE~~ ANDY,

I never ~~~~ "Saturday night Live" ago You're humor is an insul such a good show. Go back Quit, give-up.

november 24, 1974

Dear Sis,

I humbly request the opportunity to rip Andy Kaufman's legs off! My experience is as follows; I practiced for the bout by wrestling my 260 pound step-father.

My feeble minded foe hasn't a chance, He's clumsy and slow-witted, whereas, I am faster, smarter and more supple, Once more in the name of women and sports fans everywhere let me put an end to his childish gibber!

Sincerely,
Vanessa (Killer Rabbit) Welch

Andy Kaufman –

I can beat you, because my brain has been lifting weights (mainly in the form of esoteric books) for <u>years</u>.

And when you see my body, you won't <u>wanna</u> win! Cynthia E.

Andy Kaufman
P.O. Box 860
Radio City Station
NYC 10019

Dear Mr. Kaufman —

I challenge you! Wrestle me on live television...
unless you're scared! Not only am I a woman and therefore
possessing of a body far superior to your wimpy frame, but I
am a woman among women. I have youth, I have strength,
I have healthy sexual energy in abundance. What have you
got? Show me, if you have the guts. I guarantee I'll have
you on the floor before you're even finished looking at me.
You don't think I can do it? Just look at the hold I've got
on that guy in the picture... my grip is so good I'm still
holding on! But don't think I'm not mean. I am. Also
tough, smart and invincible. You couldn't beat me in my
sleep!

I'll bet your hesitating. I'll bet you're figuring your
chances. But you haven't got a chance! I'll twist you up
in a knot so tight you'll need surgery to straighten →

yourself out. I'll make you sorry you were born, like everyone else is. I'll teach you a lesson in the superiority of women you'll _never_ forget.

I'm waiting for your answer. If it's "no", I'll know for sure that you're the chickenshit coward I've always known you were. Come on, coward, take the gauntlet I've thrown down.

Accept the challenge, you male insect.

Take your chances with me, you supreme specimen of sexual inadequacy.

Gather your strength and prepare, you cowering slime.

And say goodbye ~~the~~ to the world!

Claire R.

STRONGEST, MEANEST, TOUGHEST, FASTEST
REAL WOMAN IN THE WORLD!

Houston, Texas 71081

Dear Andy Kaufman, I Hate Your Guts!
© 2009 Lynn Margulies

PROCESS

Process Media
1240 W. Sims Way
Suite 124
Port Townsend, WA 98368
www.processmediainc.com

designer: Lissi Erwin/Splendid Corp.
editors: Jodi Wille + Lissi Erwin

Printed in China

ISBN: 978-1-934170-08-3

10 9 8 7 6 5 4 3 2 1